THE LEETER
SPIAKING SINGLISH
3

T0017561

THE LEETER
SPIAKING
SINGLISH

BOOK 3:
LOANWORDS

Gwee Li Sui

Marshall Cavendish
Editions

Published in 2022 by Marshall Cavendish Editions
An imprint of Marshall Cavendish International

A member of the
Times Publishing Group

Other Marshall Cavendish Offices:
Marshall Cavendish Corporation, 800 Westchester Ave, Suite N-641, Rye Brook, NY 10573, USA • Marshall Cavendish International (Thailand) Co Ltd, 253 Asoke, 16th Floor, Sukhumvit 21 Road, Klongtoey Nua, Wattana, Bangkok 10110, Thailand • Marshall Cavendish (Malaysia) Sdn Bhd, Times Subang, Lot 46, Subang Hi-Tech Industrial Park, Batu Tiga, 40000 Shah Alam, Selangor Darul Ehsan, Malaysia

Marshall Cavendish is a registered trademark of Times Publishing Limited

National Library Board, Singapore Cataloguing in Publication Data

Name(s): Gwee, Li Sui, 1970-
Title: The Leeter Spiaking Singlish. Book 3, Loanwords / Gwee Li Sui.
Description: Singapore : Marshall Cavendish Editions, 2022.
Identifier(s): ISBN 978-981-5009-65-1
Subject(s): LCSH: English language--Variation--Singapore. | English language--Spoken English--Singapore. | English language--Dialects--Singapore. | English language--Singapore--Foreign words and phrases.
Classification: DDC 427.95957--dc23

Printed in Singapore

CONTENTS

TERIMA KASIH!

ME AND MY SISTER got take different paths in life. We started out in the same kilat but now la tee too MacRitchie Primary School – which si geenas from Braddell lah, Pei Chun lah, Poi Ching lah, Kheng Cheng lah, Heng A Khe Bong lah, First Toa Payoh lah (yes, unker is shaming you all!) kio the Monyet School. I remember my sister whacking a few of those who would cucuk me in our school bus.

Then, as fate had it, we kena sent to different secondary schools. She turned into this Ah Lian who could whole day sing pop songs while I became a banana bookworm. Her kawan-kawan oso not same-same as mine – although, looking back, all of us quite obiang lah. But sama-sama grow up meant we two must keep bridging the cultural worlds that were pulling us apart.

Now we both unker and auntie liao. Our spiaking has become a lot more zai only because we long-long got accept the importance of Singlish. Without Singlish, how to even communicate? Use hands and feet meh? So my this volume of *The Leeter Spiaking Singlish* is dedicate to Gwee Li Choo, who remains hampalang I cannot be. If I is the Luke Skywalker of Singlish, then this lao chio bu is Leia.

INTRODUCTION

Book Three liao. If you still asking what Singlish is, then you very the cannot make it. But unker is a nice guy lah. Unker will explain to you free of charge – again. Singlish is Singapore's steady pom pi pi unofficial language. It is what happens when you let hampalang languages and dialects spoken on our Leeter Red Dot campur-campur. After a few generations, you get this lawa thing go anywhere is can hear one.

The campurring, I must stress, is key hor. Why ah? Because, while my definition of Singlish quite standard, not everybawdy acherly unnerstans what it means. You no believe? Got ever hear kukujiaos say "Eh, so much Melayu is more Mat talk than Singlish leh"? Or "Use so leeter England, sounds more like Hokkien"? Or "Singlish is when poor peepur try to spiak England"?

Teruk siol. All these kuas should balik kampung and – in our champion TV character Phua Chu Kang's words – use their brains. They no makan nasi *campur* before meh? On the same plate got nasi but oso other different dishes, tio bo? So say Singlish involves cam-purring is mean what? Walao eh, dunno why explain to sotongs always must go until so basic one. But nem-mind! Unker is a nice guy.

This quality of being chapalang is, in fact, how Singlish can stay gerek. It is what keeps its speakers stim about words, especially new ones koped for the sake of changing reality. It is oso what keeps its normal words fluid, changing in meaning lah, speowling lah, usage lah. We who spiak Singlish are thus more open about who to spiak with – because a porous language is more welcoming mah!

My this humble book series *The Leeter Spiaking Singlish* is celebrate such a mo tak teng language one. It acherly grew out of my original 2017 publishing sensation *Spiaking Singlish*. While that book was sibeh popular, unker fewls, structure-wise, it was quite all over the place lah. That was, to be fair, part of the fun. But now unker must update and expand the material liao. So hampalang at the same time re-arrange lor.

Remember this volume is focused on loanwords nia. Nonid to cow peh cow bu about why no this or

that – you can ownself go check whether earlier vol-
umes got cover oredi anot. Or just nanti until I write
summore, can? But simi is this category kio loanwords?
Loanwords are basically borrowed words lor. They are
words kapo-ed from other languages and dialects and
used with sikit to geero changes to them.

But, before you kay kiang go all woke and hentam
Singlish for cultural appropriation, let me stir summore.
Loanwords are *not* a Singlish thing ler. Hampalang languages are got such loaning and borrowing one, which
naturally follow the meeting of any two languages.
Show unker a language that consperm bo loanword,
and unker will show you a language bo lang use liao, a
matied language.

Yes, the banking metaphors can be quite mis-
leading. When one language borrows from another
language, the source does not acherly rugi because
where got lose anything? Borrowed words oso will not
later give back – and that is expected. After all, how
to even return siol? A loanword is not macam a library
book. It is more like the money a gambling addict
utangs you.

Oso, this taking from another language is not a bad
thing mah. Some peepur call it stealing from the poor,
but these jokers really bo tak chek. In history, it is often
the languages of tua ki or atas and lawa communities

11

whose ideas and words got influence other languages. So, while last time German tribes got kapo a lot of words from the Romans, very the few German words acherly entered Latin.

With Singlish, the main languages it kapos from are ownself kapo kings. Tamil's "thavaranai" and "veranta" – meaning tavern and verandah – came from where ah? Portuguese, specifically "taverna" and "veranda" (which England oso kapo-ed). Tamil peepur makan kokis and lim kōfii, but "cookie" and "coffee" are from "koekje" and "koffie" in Dutch. Which, in turn, went back one to German and the other to Arabic.

Tamil's "kaju", the word for cashew, is kapo from Portuguese's "caju" while "kaccān" came clearly from "kacang" in Melayu lor. "Māṅkōsṭīṉ", for mangosteen, is oso from Melayu, from "manggustan". Now, note interestingly "mangosteen" and "mango" are same-same but different. The latter, "mangga" in Melayu, is acherly – surplise! – from Tamil's "māṅkāy" or Malayalam's "māṅṅa".

Hampalang Melayu days of the week came from Arabic: Ahad, Isnin, Selasa, Rabu, Khamis, Jumaat, and Sabtu. The word for history, "sejarah", is oso from Arabic, from "shajarah" for tree. From England, Melayu got take "narrative" to create "naratif" and "science" to make "sains". While ang moh "tea" is from "teh" in Hokkien or Melayu, Melayu's "biskut" is from England's "biscuit".

We can heow summore! Mandarin for apple is what ah? "Píngguǒ" (苹果), from Sanskrit's "bimbā". Nirvana, "nièpán" (涅槃), is oso from Sanskrit. Peepur always say our local cheena word "bāshā" (巴刹), for market, came from Melayu, but "pasar" is from "bazar" in Persian, from which England got "bazaar". Then got computing words like "bókè" (博客) lah, "hēikè" (黑客) lah, "jíkè" (极客) lah – for "blog", "hacker", and "geek"...

Even England, the world's most yaya international language, is a champion kapo king wor! Agak-agak eighty per cent of its vocab is from somewhere else one. England kopes from as many as 350 languages – from Latin lah, French lah, German lah, Italian lah, Spanish lah, Portuguese lah, Russian lah; from Arabic lah, Persian lah, Yiddish lah, Sanskrit lah, Hindi lah, Urdu lah, Mandarin lah, Japanese lah, Melayu lah, Maori lah; from Afrikaans lah, Swahili lah, Zulu lah. Even Singlish it oso got gasak!

So England's "cash" and "curry" are from Tamil's "kācu" and "kari". From Melayu's "kampung", it made two words: "kampong" you know, but oso "compound"! Cheena peepur got contribute to England "feng shui" and "kung fu", but oso – you know anot? – "brainwash", from "xǐnǎo" (洗脑). "Ketchup", from Melayu's "kicap", acherly came from Hokkien's "kê-chiap" (鮭汁)!

From Singlish, England got kapo words like "ang moh" lah, "shiok" lah, "lepak" lah, "Ah Beng", "blur" lah, "helicopter" lah, "killer litter" lah. You can ownself go check the *Oxford England Dictionary* and see with your own bak chew. The sotongs who then ngeh-ngeh argue these words not Singlish but Melayu or Hokkien or even England are missing the point. England got find these words, with their specific meanings, *via* Singlish. We changed them, and now they are belong to us.

All this highlights how anybawdy who claims simi pure England is talk cock nia. England was – and remains – the world's most steady pom pi pi language campur-er. Unker will even say it became so tok kong because of this talent for campurring. Meanwhile, a lot of stupiak discussion surrounds Singlish. Some kay ang mohs insist, unlike England, Singlish is low-crass rojak. Then they happy-happy enunciate words like "enfant terrible" and "agent provocateur" the *French* way.

The bestest kay ang mohs can use words like "cale-fare" and think those are ang moh words. Wah piang eh. One day, all these goondus will make me vomit blood until I mati. In this book, we will tikam-tikam look hard at a dozen of loanwords. Of course, along the way, we sure will talk about a lot more one. But hor, if you wan to ngeow to the max, acherly almost hampalang Singlish words are loanwords lah. Think about eet.

1
WORK, CABUT, LIVE

UNKER'S HEART very the fragile. It can pecah easily one. For example, whenever I got hear some young Sinkie say at the end of a siong workday he or she pang kang or thng chu, my heart piak liao. The first Hokkien phrase is mean to finish work while the second one means to go home. Their use is not salah here – unlike, say, "balik kampung", which does *not* mean to thng chu hor. But why even use them?

What happened to the good ol' times when peepur got enough cow sense to know why they zho kang? What happened to unnerstanding that work and life not same-same and all the hours you pia in the office was *for* life – which would start once you pang kang? Dun peepur these days fewl shiok to announce loud-loud

"Mai tu liao! Time to cabut!", which agak-agak means "Dun dilly-dally anymore! Let's *escape*"?

Maybe got pockets of workers still use "cabut", but, in general, we not saying it enough lah. This is sibeh telling and chum. The Melayu word is mean to pull out or extract and should be pronounced, if you dunno, "cha-boot" hor. But Singlish speakers always chin chye use and lagi chin chye speowl and pronounce one. So sometimes you may get simi "chabot" lah, "charbok" lah, what have you.

The more tok kong point is that "cabut" needs three bodily expressions to say one. First is you must kay-kay you hurrying, macam got no time and need to cepat-cepat pack up and go. Then you must look at least sikit guilty or paiseh you cannot stay on and pia with your fellow comrades. Last is to show you acherly fewl happy like bird or relieved that – heng ah! – you got find a way out.

These three expressions are must chut in order one. The pattern conveys you eh zho nang and human-ises you as well as your working environment. What hurrying shows is you unnerstan urgency and can be responsible. Guilt or paisehness shows your workplace got gotong royong and you appreciate eet. Pleasure or relief reveals you got your own life and reminds others to oso wake up their ideas.

How much of this pattern you chut is sincere acherly no one can tell. After all, how to even prove if a cabutter fewls a certain way anot? Irregardless of intention, all three expressions must happen one. So, say you utang money and must hide from an ah long (not to be confused with Ah Loong, our respected PM), what do you tell your sayangs? Say "Sorry, I must cabut!" with these three steps lor.

"Cabut" can oso appear in guai-guai, less teruk situations, as when you must leave an office meeting to go meet a client. To cabut here may or may not mean you truly wan to be released. It does not consperm you fewl sibeh gerek about your next appointment. This ambiguity is what *lightens* the context. "Cabut" becomes a bouncy, la-dee-da way to cucuk, elak, and bo chup and yet sound polite.

"Cabut" thus got a lot of character one! Just compare it to other same-same but different Singlish terms such as "siam" and "take cover". Those two nonid a show of guilt and concern more a job you know too well can fly back in your face. By the way, "siam" is pronounced as "see-yum" and not "sai-yam" hor. It is not that last time name for Thailand – although, in our Thai-inspired dish mee siam, we oso say "see-yum".

"Siam" may mean elak, but you can use to tell peepur to move aside too. So, at a hawker centre, a server with sio dishes or a cleaner with a trolley may cow-peh "Siam ah!" Meanwhile, Singlish's "take cover" does not just mean seek shelter as in England and is from SAF one. Patrolling soldiers jump into bushes or longkangs to take cover should they sense enemies ahead.

But how are these two terms differ-ent from "cabut" neh? Well, the con-text for "siam" and "take cover" is not that final. So, in the army, there may be a lot of siamming and taking cover but bo cabutting one. You can always siam or take cover from guard duty – but who can ever cabut sial? "Cabut" assumes you got power to mai zho kang and knowledge you sure will head to a better place.

As such, the office use of "cabut" is very the tok kong wor! To cabut is a basic civvie right; it is a social freedom you have. You cannot cabut in a military or despotic setting nia. This point unker must stress for the sake of hampalang sian-looking, overworked si geenas out there. Unker needs to explain this one thing you all so geram about *not* having enough or at all: work-life balance.

You see, Sinkies always suka complain ah complain about bo time for self and family – but we got act macam we got the power to *make* time anot? Work-life balance ultimately begins with the way we think, how we ownself tell ownself what life is lah. If every work-day all you do is pang kang or thng chu, then you oredi ownself damn ownself to a kiam chye mia.

If life is just stop work and head home to rilek and tidur and next day balik to work, then you where got happening? If you dun react against this, acherly you suka having no work-life balance one. All your complaining is wayang nia. If you bo assert a vision and a sense of direction for your life, why you even deserve to be freed from sianness ah? You dowan eet!

To truly experience life, for which work is a mere means, you must focus and exersai some garangness lah. You must look forward to what comes after work, to what is *not* work. You should got identify everything else you would rather do and everywhere else you would rather be liao. You need to believe every day you zho kang is in order to cabut! Only then can you be free, Mr. Anderson.

2

MY WONDER CUM CHAPTER

SOME TIME AGO got peepur say to me the way Sinkies use "cum" ought to be considered Singlish. Unker was quite action then about it being England – because must be mah! After all, who got tak chek one deen learn it back in school? Hampalang England dictionaries oso define it as "with" in Latin. So we find beds-cum-sofas lah, mops-cum-vacuum cleaners lah, restaurants-cum-cafes lah...

But, you see, England oso got many words whose meanings change over time. Some words last time meant one thing but now is mean another thing. Once a pong a time, "brave" was refer to being how lian and not garang one. When you kio someone notti, you were saying he or she poor, got *naught*, geero, kosong, geddit?

Summore, a char bor who was buxom was super guai-guai and might not have big tetek.

Some words even got go terbalik such as "egregious", which acherly meant sibeh good last time. Now it means sibeh bad, *terrihorbly* bad – but why liddat? Sama-sama with "awful", which used to mean full of awe. Now you go tell your boss he or she is awful lah. You try. And, believe it anot, a bully was once your sayang wor! So William Shakespeare got a blur soldier who angkat bola Henry V by saying "I love the lovely bully".

Lagi more words collect layers of meanings to the point they mean different things in different contexts. So, when someone tells you go fly kite high-high, "high" here means, errr, high. But "high" can oso mean thani until mabok or take drugs, tio bo? (Dun take drugs hor.) "Wicked" can mean evil, but something sibeh kilat is oso wicked. Then got "gay" and "queer", whose different meanings nonid to teach you liao.

All these bring me to the word "cum" and why we must ai zai and keep up with current trends lah. Because, more and more, peepur are using it to speowl "come" – that is, semen (not seamen ah). This "come" comes (cums? I blur liao!) from the word's other verbal meaning for having an orgasm (not organism ah). It is why we arm chio macam si geenas whenever we got hear someone say "I come" or "I coming", corright?

At the same time, the England-spiaking world is following the innocent Latin word use less and less liao. If you go uni tio cum laude, it means you got – wah! – graduate with distinction. If you tio magna cum laude, you is lagi steady pom pi pi, and "summa cum laude" just makes you a chow mugger toad. If you buy stocks and hear "cum dividend", it means got a dividend lor. These are the few notchyet confusing uses.

But, in regular use nowsaday, peepur dun say "cum" when "with" or "and" can oredi. Basically, England kena streamlined lah. In fact, as far as textual usage among England speakers goes, "cum" climaxed (pun not intended) in the eighteenth century liao. *Collins England Dictionary* reveals, by the end of last century, its use got drop by over 96 per cent! Unker sure will not tio chuak if it is considered happening in Singapore nia.

In other words, to use "cum" as preposition in our day and age is aiyoyo lah. Any serious England speaker cannot fail to hear the jialat notti meaning and be stunned like vegetable. Its Latin use is technically still OK unless we dun bother with hyphens, which – alamak! – we dun. So, if many Sinkies treat "cum" as "with" and yet dun hyphenate, is this not uniquely us? Should the word then not be considered Singlish?

This kuat line of argument is what converted me lor. Its unnerstanding can oso reveal so much about us as a peepur. First, we see how all our insistence on simi Standard England has acherly caused our England to go senget from widely spoken England. We go haywire *ironically* because we so ngeow about sticking to dictionary meanings! Tell you lah: sumpah nobawdy who lives by *Oxford* or *Webster's* or *Collins* will be lagi pandai when it cums (comes?) to spoken meanings one.

Our blur sotong use shows a susah over-compensation, a wish to be lagi England than England speakers. We wan to pally-pally with ang moh culture but end up looking stupiak. I mean, why we cannot just use "with" or "and" ha? Why not "Dinner and Variety Show" or "National Day Concert with Prize-Giving Ceremony"? No, we must kay kiang create posters that tembak with "Minister's Opening Cum Dumpling Festival".

What to do? Sinkies suka aksi borak and end up liddat lor. We wan to sound tua ki and end up sounding tua ki in a goblok way. Orbigood! This is funny oso because we acherly think ours is double-confirmed Queen's England. So I open the newspaper and see ads for "receptionists cum secretaries". I go jalan-jalan and see a town council banner for "Sports Carnival Cum Three on Three Cup".

A real ang moh reading all these public messages sure will stress until lao big sai. Only a kay ang moh can tidak apa about the wordings being even at odds with our otherwise conservative society. He or she will terbalik think using "cum" shows he or she got tak chek or very the atas. For the rest of this chapter, unker will kolaveri about these kuas — because I sibeh buay tahan them!

To be sure, kay ang mohs are not same-same as ang mohs hor. Ang mohs are basically Westerners, whom some still kio Mat Salleh or orang putih – that is, white peepur. Meanwhile, kay ang mohs and jiak kentangs are same-same but different. The latter are England-heliucated locals so soaked in ang moh culture they dunno, or lose touch with, their ethnic languages and cultures. So they oso ang moh pai one.

ABCs, or American-born cheena, are a type of jiak kentangs. Last time cheena jiak kentangs were oso called bananas – because yellow outside but white inside mah. These days, when you mention bananas, peepur tend to think of something else. (So jialat.) With jiak kentangs, at least you know their England very the can. They oso often fewl a sense of loss, unlike these kay ang mohs.

Kay ang mohs are sibeh interesting ler. They think, because they got tak chek or got ang moh kakis or, best, an ang moh accent, their England is automatically tok kong. (But their accent is dunno pick up from where one!) With this half past six England, they then go around see others no up and aksi borak. What kay ang mohs most famously suka hentam is Singlish.

From morning to night, kay ang mohs declare England da bestest and Singlish koyak. They complain ah complain about how hawkers and service staff buay spiak good England lah, how this will cause Singapore to rugi lah, how we oredi becoming a fishing village again lah. But the rest of us listen to them talk cock and think, "Eh, how come their England so funny one?" One clue to spot these kuas is this "cum, cum, cum" business lor.

3

ESKEW ME, ARE YOU A GOONDU?

How DO I CALL thee dumb-dumb in Singlish? Let unker count the ways hor. "Dumb-dumb" is one, and "cockanathan" is another. Last time we oso said some-one got a screw loose, macam he or she a robot. This phrase appears in Sinhalese too, so maybe more than one source? When you investigate, acherly many lao Singlish words got complicated history one. So peepur who suka how lian claim this or that word is from their culture must look beyond lah.

We oso say "duh" in Singlish – which is not same-same as ang mohs' "duh" hor. Theirs is a sarcastic response, like "This is so simper – duh!" Ours is an adjective, like "Eh, you very the duh hor?" It is what

the Hokkiens call "thur" and mocks how a slow-witted person may spiak. The muttered "burr, burr, burr" in that ang moh poet William Wordsworth's "The Idiot Boi" is something liddat. So mean, corright?

Nowsaday, a certain Singlish modification of the word "stupid" is lagi popular. We say "stupiak" to describe duh-ness that is so jialat peepur wan to piak the kua. "Piak" got a few Singlish meanings one. It can mean slap but oso pecah, as when an ah pui sit on my iPad and it piaks. But "piak-piak" is the sound of skin slapping during sex – so dun anyhowly go "piak, piak, piak" ah!

From Melayu got "bangang", but we use more "bodoh", which is said by aiming a whole hand at the addressee or rapping his or her forehead. "Bodoh" can be a noun or an adjective, and so both "That bodoh is our MP" and "Brudder, dun bodoh, can?" can. If you wan to wayang scolding somebawdy, you can oso cow-peh "Bodoh peh kambing!", which means a stupiak goat but more drama.

"Gila" is another shiok Melayu word and can mean crazy or stupiak. This one was made famous by a classic Malaysian *Mad*-inspired funny magazine kio *Gila-Gila* from the 1970s and 1980s. That publication was once sibeh widely read even by Sinkies who deen know Melayu – because got a lot of solid ang kong! A gila person can oso be called a gila monster, after a type of lizard native to North America.

From Indonesia came "goblok", which ah laos still suka use. The Javanese word is acherly "goblog", but no Sinkie speowls it liddat one. It is steady to note that, while Indonesians got other same-same words like "tolol" lah, "bego" lah, "dungu" lah, "bebal" lah, it is "goblok" that entered Singlish. Why neh? Saya tak tahu – maybe because it echoes the England "blockhead"?

From Mandarin came "kua", from "shǎguā" (傻瓜), or agak-agak silly melon. I suppose a kua is a melon because he or she is thick mah. Of hampalang cheena dialects, Hokkien got give Singlish the most ways of insulting somebawdy. "Gong" means stupiak, and "gong-gong" means stupefying. An ah gong is not same-same as Melayu's agong, who is a king, or ah kong, who is a grandfather. This one is a bodoh!

There is oso, from Hokkien, "siow ting tong", which I can part-explain nia. "Siow" means gila while "ting tong" sounds more like a doorbell than a proper word. Unker got no idea what it is, let alone why a ting tong is siow. Why ah? Maybe it suggests nobawdy is home in the head or refers to the Ting and Tong families? (The Tings and Tongs I know not that siow... or maybe sikit.)

Then got "kukujiao", which acherly refers to the leeter bird in a cuckoo clock, the one every hour pops out and goes "ku ku". Well, in Singlish, this is a euphemism for a guy's leeter brudder. When someone calls you a kukujiao, it means you either very the cock or you sibeh kuai lan. You screw up so much you gone case liao. I find this insult somehow less rude compared to "kotek" lah, "kunji" lah, "pundek" lah, "puki" lah. (I not teaching you bad words ah.)

Finally, how to overlook Tamil's most tok kong contribution to Singlish siol? "Goondu" is the most kilat of kilat Singlish words to mean dumb-dumb. It was made popular by that Ah Ma of Singlish, Sylvia Toh

Paik Choo, through her 1980s bestsellers *Eh, Goondu!* and *Lagi Goondu!* one. (Sidetrack: it is Paik Choo and not Piak Choo hor. Warned you before dun anyhowly "piak, piak" liao – wait later her fans anger come and piak choo!)

Although some claim this word is from "gundu" in Melayu, meaning hard and heavy, both are tied to the Tamil game of goli one. Goli is, in England, called marbles, and a goondu is that big, white goli used to knock the other leeter golis. I think only those of us who grew up playing goli will know lah. Goli was why our school maths questions used to always involve Kok Meng's, Ali's, and Muthu's marbles, tio bo?

But, you know, peepur who know Tamil can con-sperm tell you an interesting problem with our Singlish use. "Goondu" is mean fatso and not dumb-dumb ler. In the history of our multiculturalism, somehow the word use got change radically – from pui-pui to stupiak. It

WHY YOU SO GOONDU?

is like how Tamil's "auta" oso got broaden from bedek or kay to lao ya. Why ah? Maybe because "goon" kena read as England, and so "goondu" became linked to a goblok.

No wonder foreign Tamils gong-gong whenever they hear Sinkies call folks of all shapes and sizes goondus lah! This change in meaning, to be sure, is normal with loanwords in any language one. Even in England, the adjective "nice" deen use to be so nice. It came from the Latin "nescius", which means... stupiak. So, if I say you a nice person, last time Romans would have thought I called you goondu wor!

At least Tamil words like "aiyoh", "mama", "annan" (or "anneh"), "thambi", "thani", and "kolaveri" mean same-same in Singlish. But the change with "goondu" got a practical use ler. It can reveal whether a Tamil speaker is born and bled here or lived here long-long or is visiting nia. Say A calls B a goondu, but the latter fewls sibeh offended for the salah reason, looking – kua kua – lagi goondu...

"Goondu" is distinct from another class of words whose original meanings non-Tamil speakers dunno but should know lah. This class includes "samudera", which means sea; "thanggam", which means gold; and "kovan", which can refer to a herdsman, a king, or the Hindu Lord Shiva. Ask any tidak apa, Tamil-ignorant

Sinkie what they mean, and you will hear LRT and MRT stations... which is not salah. But, alamak, sibeh goondu leh!

4

DUN BE A
CHOW MUGGER!

You CANNOT SUKA-SUKA ownself call ownself a
true-blue Sinkie one. We Sinkies got our own yard-
stick for deciding whether your claim is got pakay anot.
One criterion is you must got survive our world-crass
education system. You must have kena from fierce
teachers and lagi fierce parents before. You must have
kena stressed like siow by piles of homework until you
kooned on them.

This criterion got lagi more sub-criteria, so unker
has barely started. You must know all about school
ranking lah, the quest for model answers lah, Ten-Year
Series lah, question-spotting lah, exam smarts lah. You
must got know someone who was sibeh chow kuan,
if you ownself not this auta person. You must got go

after-school tuition while, at the same time, worry about simi ECA or CCA points. On and on the list goes.

Deen even that last time education ministar Ng Chee Meng tell our students to grow an "entrepreneurial dare" to "chiong"? By "entrepreneurial dare", he meant not so much to become a towkay as to be innovative. And, by "chiong", he did not mean to go clubbing and thani until mabok hor. That is *one* meaning, but what was meant is to ownself push ownself to the limit, to pia macam your life depends on eet.

Anyone who got ever see a classmate chiong – or ownself got chiong – will know this hantu of a creature called the mugger. A mugger is got nothing to do with a muggle from J. K. Rowling's Harry Potter books because sometimes you even wonder if the former is human anot. A mugger is more a particular breed of young learner who will grow up to be a particular breed of Sinkie.

The word oso does not mean same-same as in England hor. It does not describe a robber. It rather follows the Singlish verb "mug", which is the equivalent of England's "mug *up*". Both refer to absorbing as much information as possible in a sibeh short time. But you wonder why ang mohs can say "John mugs up on pure maths over the holidays" but neh arrive at saying "John is a mugger" leh. This is why Singlish is so tok kong!

Top schools in Singapore are chock-full of muggers one. In fact, unless a school can encourage a culture of mugging, it cannot become a top school. These champion students are so kilat they know hampalang answers even before a class lesson begins. Hampalang homework set by the teachers they oredi complete religiously... *and more*. They always score As for assignments lah, tests lah, exams lah – but A-minus cannot ha!

SO CHOW MUGGER TOAD.

A mugger is bo personality one, so you dowan to sit next to one unless to copy his or her answers. But beware hor: a mugger is very the protective over his or her kilatness and will neh let you copy so easily! If he or she spots you, he or she sure will repork teacher, and then you habis. A mugger finds his or her greatest pleasure in beating everyone else academically. This is why he or she often got a kiam pah face.

To be sure, a mugger is not same-same as a typical nerd or geek ler. A nerd or geek may be antisocial and cannot friend-friend type, but at least he or she is truly pandai. The nerd's or geek's passion for knowledge is fixated on one subject nia. It is this excessive commitment to knowing that makes him or her ki siow. You can see all the shiok luanness burn in his or her bak chew macam BBQ.

But the mugger is not pandai one. He or she can only process a lot of information fast-fast. This very ability is gained through daily mechanical practice, through memorising chunks of text lah, finding formulas for answers lah – macam how you train an anjing to cycle or a monyet to dance. A mugger is not interested in knowledge per se. All he or she wans is to win-win-win nia!

"Mugger" may seem to be a mere label, but it is a tok kong humanising word. It is first and foremost a curse used to jaga others against what they may become. So often peepur take turns to call one another a mugger so as to save their kawan-kawan from the hantus or kakas our education system are turning them into. There *is* power in peer pressure – so today you is a mugger, and tomorrow it is me.

To cry "You chow mugger!" or "Dun be a chow mugger!" or "Stop mugging lah!" is thus sibeh bagus. Life truly happens when you are *not* whole day chow mugging. Then you got time to go smell the roses lah, play goli or football or computer games lah, enjoy cosplaying lah. You can read all the fun books and not textbooks or assessment books. You can go pak tor or beo char bors at the malls.

But, if someone keeps mugging despite every warning from his or her kawan-kawan, soon he or she will gone case liao. He or she will become that embodiment of mugging, a champion mugger we call the mugger toad. Now, the mugger is called "mugger" for objective reasons nia. To be subjective, we tend to mock this kua as a chow mugger or a mugger toad or – best – a chow mugger toad.

The "toad" reference is point to being a toady, one who sar kars an atas or powderful figure. In "mugger toad", this sense got lagi teruk because the authority is not merely the teacher or the parents hor. It includes the school lah, the whole education system lah, the status quo with all its chum-ness. A toady is macam a goondu or a sabo king in that they are all chow turtles. (Dun ask me why, in Singlish, a toad is a type of turtle.) But a chow mugger toad is a lot *more* than a chow turtle!

Let unker tell you why. A mugger toad may not be pandai, but he or she knows well what he or she is doing. His or her book smarts acherly hides his or her world smarts. The mugger is studying basically to angkat bola peepur who can sayang him or her and empower him or her next time to huat in a manner that does not change the way the world is. When a mugger toad grows up, he or she will become a sibeh familiar kind of Sinkie to other Sinkies.

5

IS "RUGI" OR "LUGI" AH?

KAWAN-KAWAN, first thing to unnerstan by now is every language got loanwords one. Every language got words it kapos from other languages and change ah change according to how its users spiak. This is nothing unique since we hampalang can agree language got power mah. Power means can affect not just speakers of a language but oso those who come in contact with it, corright?

So, if some si geenas no appreciate loanwords and suka cow-peh about Singlish stealing from other languages, you tell them go fly kite lah. Or invite them tolong please go tak chek and dun whole day ownself malu ownself. Any Ah Ter Ah Kow can talk cock sing song, but real commitment to language and culture is mean what? Is mean can go learn properly about how these exist mah.

Singlish absorbing words and changing their sounds lah, speowlings lah, meanings lah, is normal one. Melayu, for example, oso got do this. England's "taxi" became "teksi"; Latin's "scholē", meaning leisure, became "sekolah"; and Hokkien's "diam" became, well, "diam". Mandarin oso is a kapo king. "Champagne" became "xiāngbīn" (香槟); "hamburger" became "hàn-bǎobāo" (汉堡包); and "kampung" became "gānbǎng" (甘榜).

Second thing to unnerstan is sikit cheemer. It is this: until a loanword is stable, it can have multiple pro-nunciations, speowlings, and even meanings one. But who stabilises ah? Users lor – and over time. Especially when no central authority exists to regulate, this pro-cess to fix a word can take sibeh long. We should acherly fewl shiok that Singlish got a life beyond any one group's control wor!

As such, variation is really nothing to wah about. It follows use and can even happen *within* each language. So American and British England are not spiak same-same: "toe-may-toe", "toe-mah-toe"; "poe-tay-toe"... "poe-tay-toe". "Lieutenant" is pronounced as "loo-ten-ant" in one and "lef-tenant" in the other. Melayu oso got Malaysian cum Sinkie version and Indonesian version plus last time system and current system for speowling from the 1970s.

With the word "lugi", the original Melayu form is just "rugi" lah. "Rugi" means lose, often in the financial sense. We Singlish speakers suka anyhowly pronounce – because multiculturalism is a lot of give and take mah. Some peepur who hear "lugi" may make it a racial issue, but unker thinks nonid everything kolaveri one. Which language neh do this thing to another can please cast the first batu?

In Singlish, sound change happens all the time! Yes, "roti" became "loti"; "hentam" became "humtum"; "terbalik" became "tombalik". But "shagged" got become "shack" and "jiak lat" "jialat"; "steady poon pee pee" is becoming "steady pom pi pi". All these forms, to be sure, still co-exist, and to insist on one is to demand regulation. It is to wan the gila thing of controlling a bo centre, dynamic, la-dee-da process.

Controlling is sibeh naive lah. Sound change is to suit how a language articulates. It oso happens out of play, as when "on" produced "onz". This can be in the form of a double meaning, as when "speak" became "spiak", which oso means flamboyant. But some words suay-suay lose their nuances with time. "Sekali" was "scully" last time because of the popularity of that chio FBI agent from the TV series *The*

Is "Rugi" or "Lugi" ah?

X Files. Today's millennials will ki siow when they see it speowlt liddis.

How "rugi" became "lugi" may not be because, supposedly, cheena peepur cannot make "r" sound hor. (Walao eh, sometimes unker no unnerstan those who talk racist in order to cow-peh about racism.) It may simply be that "lugi" got carry the sound "lose" and thus involves a wordplay. This is macam how the word "goblok" is speowlt liddis, and not the original "goblog", to show up the word "block" mah.

Then oso got the point that "lugi" is made distinct from "rugi" to show up its sikit different Singlish use. OK lah, I can see where this argument is coming from. The word is acherly sibeh lao, and it is tok kong because it has helped manifest the typical mindset of generations of Sinkies liao. This makes it comparable with that all-time kilat Sinkie description: "kiasu". In fact, "kiasu" is mean afraid to rugi, tio bo?

We Sinkies cannot help fewling this kind of fear one. "Rugi" is primal to us. As private beings, we think all the time in terms of huats and losses as life is sibeh short and Singapore is sibeh small. So, unless we gasak every chance we get to huat, somebawdy else lagi hunger will come along and – to quote Ah Loong – "steal our lunch". Then we rugi. No wonder ngeowness and gianness are become part of our psyche lah!

The dark side of all this is how we end up always worrying maybe we kena ketuk by life. Ang mohs catch no ball about this aspect of us and think our chiwren are good at maths thanks to our world-crass education system. *No lah!* Every born-and-bled Sinkie is kilat at counting money one, what with GST lah, HDB prices lah, CPF lah, MediSave lah, and so on training our monyet brains all day.

In fact, since young, Smiley the POSB squirrel got set us thinking into our old age liao. It got teach us the virtue of being kiam and invite us to squirrel away (geddit?) that one dollar we could have bought two bowls of kway teow soup with. "Zho simi?" or "What you doing, dey?" I would hear it spiak soft-soft into my ears. "Forget recess lah! You put your money in my bank sure won't lugi one!"

This was how my – and so many others' – adventure not to lugi in life began. In school, in love, at work, at sales, on holiday, we all got keep fighting lugi-ing. So, despite "lugi" and "rugi" looking interchangeable, acherly "lugi" got a very the specific use. You can normally lose anything – barang-barang lah, kakis lah, jobs lah, races lah, faces lah – but "lugi" has a calculative sense nia. Why ha? Because Singapore lor.

Consider: if you lose your iPhone, you will say you lugi meh? No, corright? You only lugi when you must buy another phone for losing your previous one. If you got see a car accident, you got lugi meh? Lives may be lost, but you neh lugi – unless you the driver, then nonid to say lah. For anybawdy else, if you dun chop-chop kalipok go and buy 4D with the plate lumber, you may lugi!

"Lugi" is therefore interesting because often got no one other than ownself you lugi-ing to. When your Ah Lian fashion shop at Bugis uplorry as you pok kai cannot pay rent, you got lugi to that gian property owner or other shops meh? You just tell peepur you lugi – and your plight is understooded liao! You lose in the overall sense of well-being you as a kiasu Sinkie truly deserves in life.

Or take those very the eng jokers who can queue three or four hours for Michelin-starred hawker makan. You think they got consider all the precious time they will not be getting back meh? They neh one! Because the gain they gian makes them imagine they champion winners liao. In fact, when at long last they get their spreads of shiok dishes, their one thought – besides "Wah, looks good!" – is what? "Heng I neh stupiak go restaurant and lugi!"

6
I ROJAK, YOU PRATA

OTHER COUNTRIES MAY how lian about their culture or history or freedoms, but we in Singapore fewl yaya about our makan. It is not just because our hawker culture made it as UNESCO's dunno what Intangerine Cultural Heritage hor. Makan is always on our minds one. A normal Sinkie thinks about makanning when he or she is not makanning in a kopitiam lah, a hawker centre lah, a food court lah, or snacking at work or home.

In fact, Sinkies dun just makan – we *wallop* our makan. We happy-happy whack eet. "Wallop" and "whack" are violent action verbs that capture all the passion we bring to this task. It proves one thing: why our Gahmen is salah when it keeps saying Sinkies not hunger enough to succeed. Kong simi? We are *always* hunger – at least for mum-mum, *our* mum-mum, lah!

So has Sinkie makan culture gone on to affect the way we spiak with one another? Aberden? Foreigners may often call Singapore's kilat mix of different races and cultures a melting pot, but we prefer to call it rojak ler. Rojak chum-chums slices of pineapple lah, cucumber lah, you char kway lah, and tops them with kacang bits to create something sweet, sour, and spicy – all at once. It is the perfect metaphor of us!

Singapore is quintessential rojak. "Rojak", from the Javanese word "rujak", can oso imply a mess and describe bo system or method. So a group project becomes sibeh rojak when its members gabra and any-howly do. But, when this becomes luan until very the malu, we say it mee siam mai hum. "Mee siam mai hum" describes an unlikely mix since the sweet and sour noodle dish does not come with cockles one.

The tok kong story behind the idiom is the stuff of legends liao. Back in 2006, Ah Loong felt so suanned by that gila blogger mrbrown that he warned against talk-ing cock. "You put out a funny podcast," he said, "you talk about bak chor mee, I will say mee siam mai hum." Apparently, he meant to say "mai *hiam*" or "hold the chilli", but – alamak! – the word oredi left his mouth and became Singlish history.

What about the stuff we lim ah? To lim kopi is to drink coffee, which must be of the kopitiam brew kay ang mohs suka say taste like longkang water. Poot these peepur lah. But true-blue Sinkies oso know "lim kopi" is our code for kena detained and interrogated by mata or, worse, ISD. So, in one sense, everybawdy suka lim kopi, but, in another sense, *nobawdy* wans to if it can be helped, kum sia very much.

Then got that coklat malt drink kio Milo which Sinkies creatively use to make all kinds of shiok beverages. Got Milo peng lah, Milo dinosaur lah, Milo Godzilla lah... simi sai oso have! Milo got inspire that lao Singlish term "stylo-milo", meaning fashionable, but why is Milo stylo-milo neh? Saya tak tahu – maybe because "Milo" rhymes with "stylo"? Or it is marvellous what Milo can do for you?

YOUR REPORK SO ROJAK!

If you get that last joke, you are confirm-plus-chop vintage auntie or unker liao. Nowsaday, geenas dun use "stylo-milo" much, and so we may say that, ironically, "stylo-milo" is oredi not stylo-milo. It is sikit obiang even. "Obiang" is oso obiang. Spiaking of being stylo-milo and obiang, hair-dos can be described in terms of what we makan too. So an obasan (another obiang word) with curly hair has Maggi mee – which is not technically Sinkie, but nemmind.

Meanwhile, an unker with an Elvis perm is said to have a kalipok. "Kalipok" is another name for curry puff, and it appears again in the phrase "chop-chop kali-pok", which we use to get someone to fasterly do a task. This person should not be taking his or her time. So an army Occifer or NCO watching kan cheong recruits prepare for stand-by bunk may cow-peh repeatedly, "Chop-chop kalipok!"

You may be wondering when unker is getting to the big one, roti prata. I may be lor sor, but I is merely saving the best for last lah. Roti prata is this fried flat-bread from South India which, in Malaysia, is kio roti canai (because came from Chennai mah). The simper makan is made by flipping dough on a table until thin-thin and then cooking on a hot metal plate. You dip in vegetable or meat curry and makan... sibeh sedap one!

But "prata" in Singlish oso got a meaning unrelated to makan. The flipping action invokes flip-flopping that can happen with views and in matters of policies or strategies lor. So, when our Gahmen last time sought to control population size, it promoted messages to married couples such as "Stop at Two" or "Two is Enough". Later, it became "Have Three, or More if You Can Afford it". This is prata.

Or consider that time when a white paper (not toilet paper ah) got project a local population of 6.9 million by 2030. That vision stunned many Sinkies who ki siow and pushed back, leading to the largest public demonstration seen since independence siol! It was all sibeh malu for the Gahmen, which then had to prata and say acherly it expected a much lower lumber lah. Then Sinkies rilek lor.

Most recently, whole Singapore got rocked by very the ugerly accusations Ah Loong's di di and mei mei made on Facebook. These two were buay song with their kor kor because he allegedly prata-ed on their father's wish to raze their historic family home. The claims not true lor – but the whole episode made us Sinkies gek sim because we seriously dowan to see Ah Kong's chewren fight until liddat mah.

By now, maybe you got oredi note how "prata" can be both a noun and a verb. Yes, either way oso can! So you can say "Your prata very good!" or "You prata very good!" – *neither* involves a real prata. By the way, "prata" can oso suggest inverting the meaning of

something hor. So news that Singapore still ranks low on press freedom can always be prata-ed to say we freer than Swaziland and North Korea.

I got read online si geenas ngeh-ngeh claim the word is acherly tied to our last time Peepur's President, the late S. R. Nathan. Because they got use to call him the Prata Man one. Very the no big no small ler, these peepur! First, this claim is sibeh unkind because your politics should not be an excue to be racist. Second, it is false since "prata" – like "cockanathan", another

54

word getting the same cock – is got use long before Nathan came into office lor. ("Cockanathan" just means supreme rubbish, like how "shiokanathan" translates as supreme pleasure lor.)

To prata primarily highlights indecisive action or flexible information nia. So to be prata-ing fewls sikit malu – but it does *not* automatically mean the final state is less good or both pre- and post-prata-ing are bad. "Prata" just does not judge states per se in spite of those kukujiaos who simi sai oso politisai. So tolong hor, everybawdy: can dun mee siam mai hum and any-howly prata "prata", OK?

7

A PUMCHEK DEFENCE

AT SOME POINT in your Singlish-spiaking, you will come to a jialat discovery. You will realise many Singlish expressions acherly involve cucuking others and making them look macam goondus. Singlish seems to suka kacau peepur and chip away at their egos. It seems to suka expose peepur for their duh-ness lah, their lack of self-awareness lah, their antisocial acts lah, what have you.

This discovery is mo tak teng because you are getting to the heart of why Singlish is so shiok. It is shiok because every speaker got play a part in a truly kampung affair one. Here is gotong royong, neighbour-liness, that promotes *mutual humbling*. We Sinkies help one another wake up our ideas and dun get so yaya as to think we so perfect or always corright or cannot be a kua like other kuas.

"Pumchek" is a perfect place to unnerstan this cheem point. Like "lugi", the spiak term is a corrupted form. Its original Melayu word is "pancit", meaning punctured, which is used same-same as a flat tyre. So "tayar pancit" means "tyre punctured" lor. But "pumchek" is more than like how some who dunno Melayu speowl "macam" as "machum" or "macham" or "machiam", and "kacau" as "kachiau" or "kachiow" or "gah cheow".

To be sure, those words are kena mangled jialat-jialat *not* from ill intentions hor. We must remember Singlish is first and foremost use mouth spiak one – which means we cannot assume every Singlish speaker can read or speowl, let alone in Melayu. In fact, many regularly use words they ownself dunno are come from where one. So, with such mangling, must panchan and not always kolaveri lah.

But this word "pumchek" is got evolve until today when all its meanings cannot be reduced to "pancit" liao. It may even have gone terbalik to affect how "pancit" is being used metaphorically. You see, "pum-chek" got enlarge to mean how anything quite steady has gone out of shape or kua kua quickly or suddenly.

This deflation can be physical but oso mental or emotional or spiritual.

So "pumchek" need not involve just tyred vehicles such as bicycles lah, motorbikes lah, cars lah, buses lah, lorries lah, what have you. It is perfectly fine to say a MRT train or a Singapore River ferry pumchek. You can oso say a budget airplane pumchek – although, technically, an airplane still got tyres on its leeter wheels, but nonid to pumchek the point I is making here, OK?

Got summore. A chio bu's tao expression can pumchek when she ownself trips from her high heels. A senior civil servant's plan to restructure a department can pumchek – and so can his or her ego as a result. An election campaign can pumchek, and, when this happens, a politician's pride can pumchek too. When you conked out after a sibeh long workday, you are what? Pumchek lor.

There is no way of looking good with "pumchek" one! This word is not about having more or less: you can pumchek from both makanning too much and too leeter, corright? It is about going from zai to buay zai, from "Wah say!" to "Alamak". It captures a mood which, in lite-ra-rary (errr, cheem word!) studies, we call bathos. In this sense, the effect is same-same as "kua kua", where the word lets you fewl the joke.

"Pumchek" is same-same but different from two Hokkien terms, "lao hong" and "lao kwee". "Lao hong" agak-agak translates as lose air, and so a pancit tyre lao hong. A pack of Jack 'n Jill potato chips can oso lao hong past its expiry date – in which case the term means to go stale. So "lao hong" got this other meaning "pumchek" does not have, but, as you see, its use is strictly physical.

"Lao kwee" may agak-agak translate to the same, but it is neh literal. It specifically means kena malued until got no face to show. Both "lao kwee" and "pumchek" involve human foibles and fewlings, all meanings "lao hong" no have one. But these two are still not a fit ler. A reservist after IPPT may pumchek but not fewl lao kwee, tio bo? Terbalik, a kengster (not gangster ah) may lao kwee when kena caught, but it is his reputation that pumchek nia.

Lagi importantly, "pumchek" should not be confused with "pecah" hor. "Pecah" is mean broken and is sibeh harsh. It involves something piaked until habis cannot use liao. Unker can think of one way to helpchoo tell these two words apart. If can poke holes one, like a theory lah, a policy lah, a self-image lah, the word you wan is "pumchek". If cannot poke but can shatter, macam a dream, a rice bowl, or an argument, then use "pecah". Ho say bo?

My this half past six rule got at least one exception, and it is in the phrase "pecah lobang". (Do I dare be funny and say "pecah lobang" pecah lobang my rule?) Like "pumchek", this expression describes having made a hole – although a lobang can oso be an opportunity. But it got the added sense of an *intent* to deceive, which the pecah sabos. It thus means to be busted, to have a weakness, a secret, or a lie exposed.

Oso, while someone or something pumchek, someone or something pecah lobang another. "Pumchek" is passive whereas "pecah lobang" is active hor. So, the more excited a property agent gets in his or her sales pitch, the lagi likely he or she will pecah lobang by accident. Terbalik, you may say – alamak! – this agent's intention to sell off a koyak condo unit pumchek.

Or consider this simper cautionary tale. Razak tells his Ah Lian girlfriend Mui Mui he got OT a lot, but then a whiff of cheap perfume pecah lobang. Or you may just relate it liddis: Razak's attempt to sian Mui Mui pumchek. This is what then causes their long-time relationship to pecah. Soon after, Razak's Suzuki pumchek. For reasons Mui Mui's kawan-kawan cannot pecah lobang.

8

WE NEED TO TALK ABOUT "SHIOK"

SOME YEARS AGO, unker was asked to guest-star in a TV reality game show from India wor. (Yes, dun play-play – unker is Asian talent!) The show felt kinda like *The Amazing Race*, and I got put at a pit stop as a celebrity Singlish professor. My task was to introduce contestants to a list of Singlish words and then make them sikit wayang with some of the words they got learn.

But a few hours to learn nia – how can, corright? Naturally got a lot of maluating boo-boos lor. "Women in Singapore are so beautiful," one contestant blur-blur announced. "They are all so *shiok!*" A tiny audience made up of Sinkies diam-diam; some jaws dropped. Apa ini? It so happened my kilat Singlish list got another term: "cannot make it". This was classic cannot make it.

Tuan-tuan dan puan-puan, tolong can dun oso liddis gasak buta? Saya tak tahu what the media or Singapore Tourism Board or whatever agency has been telling visitors to Singapore, but "shiok" is fun and yet sibeh loaded one. Sure, we got use it to describe makan-ning lah, shopping lah, playing sports lah, simi sai we enjoy, but it does not mean satisfying nia. It does not just mean sedap or song or happy like bird or what have you.

How to even put this nicely siol? "Shiok" got a sense related to carnal appetite and so has sexual con-notation one. The *Oxford England Dictionary* now lists it and defines it with words like "cool", "great", "deli-cious", and "superb". It is a general term of approval to say something is ho say or steady pom pi pi. But this tok kong dictionary is still ultimately an England dictionary lah.

"Shiok", which came from Melayu, is one of those lao until cannot be more lao Singlish words. It is a vari-ant of "syok" or "syiok", as Malaysians speowl it, and means sibeh bagus. But then here disagreements begin liao. Some say "syok" is come from "seronok", for fun or happy, while others say is from "asyik", which describes kuat desire. "Asyik" got Sanskrit roots one. Still others link to the Punjabi "shauk", which expresses delight.

But the *OED* consperms as sources the Persian "šoḵ" and the Arabic "šawq" nia. Both these words make things lagi complicated because they can suggest happy lah, lawa lah, longing lah, playful lah, excited lah, exciting lah. They got relate to words for different kinds of desire – physical, emotional, and spiritual – and describe pleasure from greed and appetite to love and ecstasy.

This is why, in the study of Singlish, unker is normally less keen on word origins lor. Because what good is debating whether a word came from here or there – even if can con-firm-plus-chop? All I care about is how we spiak today and not how others who may not even spiak Singlish spiak in their own languages. Besides, since

64

cunning linguists still need to zho kang and keep digging, simi conclusion we reach is neh final enough.

But, by now, it should be clear the word "shiok" is not so innocent one. It was why, when the filem *Austin Powers 2* came to Singapore back in 1999, its longer title kena changed from *The Spy Who Shagged Me* to *The Spy Who Shioked Me*. That was a stroke of marketing genius sial! With just one word, Warner Brudders cleared our strict censors and yet kept the sense in the original RA word.

Nanti, how did that work ah? Remember, in Singlish, we dun acherly use "shiok" as a verb one. No decent Singlish speaker will say "I wan to shiok you" or "Ibu is shioking her kucing". So to make it a verb was sibeh creative because it signalled a foreign use for what was an ang moh filem mah. But it oso pointed to what real Singlish speakers knew too well, that this word got an underlying very the notti sense.

The same nuance is present in other otherwise guai-guai synonyms too. For example, "stim" is Melayu for steam. When you attend an event that is sibeh exciting, you say "Stim ah!" – or, if then somebawdy party-poops, you say he or she potong stim. But "steam" in England can oso suggest "steamy". Oso, "stim" can be short for "stimulated" or "stimulating", which again hints at sexual arousal.

Then got "song" from Hokkien. What you not happy, you say you buay song – which, for some reason, got no sexual connotation leh. But, if you fewl song and ask another "Song bo?", basically "Shiok anot?", the context defines how innocent this question acherly is. Its real meaning depends on whether you are asking, say, during a family holiday trip or after a visit to Geylang with a Lao Beng.

Now balik to my reality game show story. The reason why the contestant's use of "shiok" on Sinkie char bors is teruk is oso why its use in the title of *Austin Powers 2* is tok kong. "Shiok" cannot use on peepur – or, for that matter, living things – one. Unless, eeyer, you *do* mean you give or enjoy that kind of bodily pleasure. ("Eeyer", by the way, is how we express revulsion, as in "Eeyer, why you pick your nose and then shake hands?" It is kinda the terbalik of "shiok"?)

Dun misunnerstan me hor. By all means, say "This laksa is shiok!" or "Yoga makes me fewl shiok!" or "*Top Gun: Maverick* is one shiok movie!" We should fewl shiok about using the word to categorise what makes us fewl alive – and why not? In all these instances, the sexual meaning is at most latent nia. Its suggestiveness can even help enrich our sense of pleasure that is the point.

At the same time, we must jaga against supporting generalisations that misinform others about "shiok" being safe. And then talk cock about how Sinkies sibeh jialat got no interest in sex one. Dey, what talking you? Who told you all this? Our basic enjoyment – in makan-ning lah, watching movies lah, playing lah, whatever – is oredi tied up with sex linguistically. Hampalang is sexual!

In fact, with lines like "The massage over there is so shiok!", we see how slippery this word can get. All that conveys the speaker's innocence is his or her facial expression nia. Say it with an exaggerated look of ease or yayaness, and it means "The massage is excellent!" This is solid word-of-mouth guarantee of service excellence. But say it with a chee ko pek's look, and you may well get the place promptly raided by the vice squad.

9

THE SIAN
PHILOSOPHY

FEWLING SIAN is a sibeh real part of Sinkie life.
If this is due to us being a Leeter Red Dot, with no
gunung or natural lake and just sun and rain all year
round, I geddit lor. You can tell a born-and-bled Sinkie
from a New Citizen just by how much sianness he or
she shows on a daily basis. The Sinkie is the one who
looks less excited and more shack and got a lot to complain about one.

The word "sian" is acherly not as easy to translate
as some kuas may claim. These peepur think it only
means bored or boring like in Hokkien – so, when the
TV got nothing other than Mediacorp dramas, you go
"Sian man". A workday is sian when you have to per-
form the same task again and again. These senses are

not salah, and being sian does involve lacking interest or finding things bo challenge one.

But, when your Wi-Fi connection kena sai or when McDonald's jacks up the price of McSpicy (again), you can fewl sian too. You can oso fewl sian from doing too much Zumba as well as from *not* doing Zumba. You can be sian about the PM's annual National Day Rally speech, even though his audience is always smiling and clapping like siow – but why ah? Why you fewl liddis?

"Sian" seems to have found an emotional constant across fewling bored lah, lembek lah, frus lah, pumchek lah, buay tahan lah, useless lah, powerless lah, resigned lah, disillusioned lah, cynical lah. All these got an element of sianness one! Ai say, how many England words you know can even be taken up in so many ways ha? ("Ai say" is how we Singlish speakers conversely show enthusiasm, kinda like England's "I say".)

The word "sian" must be pronounced corrightly – or you will sound sibeh cock hor. You should neh say it like in the line "Dun sian char bor lah!", which agak-agak translates as "Dun dupe that woman!" That "sian" is a verb that ends with a sharp, hovering tone. It means to bedek or to con someone naive. A master in the art of sianning is kio a sian tow or a tua pow sian – literally a lying cannon.

The "sian" I is talking about is not that "sian". It is oso not a noun, the sense of which describes a cheena fairy or celestial being. The noun form is pronounced with a lagi sharp and high ending. A sian is typically immortal and buay mati one. So, when someone zho kang until bo take makan breaks, you can say he or she wans to zho sian, that is, become a heavenly creature.

All these three forms of "sian" – "sian" as adjective, verb, and noun – are wholly unrelated words. Our "sian" in focus got a kilat, self-actuating pronunciation. It pulls downwards to a low key macam an echo in a dark, cheem well. When you say "sian", you should oredi fewl sian, as though you kena a bout of monotony and finality. "Sian" is an emotive word although the emotion is ironically macam you fewl lembek, bo lat, to emote.

Got how many ways you can say you sian ah? Sianness, to be sure, is got gradation one – so dun anyhow-anyhow hor. When it is mild, you just remark "Sian" or "Sian man" or say it straightforwardly, as in "Man, I fewl sian". Then the next stage got "So sian", "Damn sian", "Kay sian", and, in the most kuat case, "Sibeh sian!" This last one is agak-agak macam cowpehing "I'm freaking sian!"

An older generation may oso say "Sian jit puah" – which means too sian by half. "Sian leh" is said when

you buay song with something you notchyet experience but must face. It registers your reluctance. "Sian sia!" is in the midst of the very experience and means "I can't freaking believe this is so sian!" Then got "Sianz", which is more a young person's existential response.

In all these uses, "sian" got nothing to do with the Melayu word "kesian", OK. Unker must clarify because now is the internet age mah. Unker is oredi seeing goondus think "kesian" and "kay sian" are same-same. *No lah!* "Kesian" is pronounced as "ke-see-un" and means to fewl sorry. It is a word to sayang with. So you can fewl kesian *and* kay sian for a burnt-out colleague – although they are distinct emotions!

At some stage, you must realise that, in sianness, we Sinkies are at our most philosophical wor. A fella who fewls sian is not experiencing listlessness nia. His or her pumchek state is curiously oso restless. This is a paradox – to be both wanting more out of life and yet resigned to living as though we got all there is liao. In sianness is a tension even within desire, where we both wan and oso not really.

What every sian Sinkie knows inside is how things should not be a certain way – and yet here we are. He or she knows is cannot fight the world and get one's way one. Life is, after all, comfortably bo meaning one mah. It is quite bodoh to think things can change or, worse, to wan things changed. And yet, inside, he or she not happy with just being zen, and the word leaves the mouth: "Sian."

Not everybawdy who uses "sian" recognises this philosophical potential even though the option to lepak and just *fewl* is, for sure, always there. Sianness is a mode of existence to simply be, to stew in tropical heat, urban blandness, and dull social and political stability.

It is a lived response to being in a dead-end paradise that acherly sustains it, and it can oddly be sibeh stim.

This is why NS remains the most steady pom pi pi gift we can give a citizen lah. Every ah boi who has to book in by 2359 or draw arms at 5 am or kena guard duty on a weekend in Tekong suddenly becomes a philosopher one. In the presence of stark reality, his mind goes blank, and he learns the lessons of going with the flow, through the motions, and into another plane of existence.

NS is this gift we should sama-sama aim to bestow on our char bors and New Citizens too, not for equality's sake – *no, no!* – but for the quality of life they can have. How much more soulful everybawdy can be siol! But, until that happy day comes, we can at least ownself console ownself with a lesser but lagi fast way of sharing sianness with all Singapore. This is to vote the PAP back into power decisively at the next General Elections.

10

TIME TO UPLORRY

COME, COME, let us talk about vehicular imagery in Singlish! Sure got a lot since everywhere you go in Singapore can see roads, roads, and more roads mah. Not only that but these roads summore every day packed until teruk-teruk with all kinds of vehicles. Got big ones lah, leeter ones lah, long ones lah, short ones lah. Then got the unker-on-bicycle anyhowly pia kind lah.

So much of Sinkie life is tied to owning a car you can drive one. Nemmind you have to pay an arm and a leg for it. You must impress your sayang lah, her family lah, your unkers and aunties lah, your kawan-kawan lah, your clients lah, and pedestrians. Who cares you bo money to buy new underwear? Oso, living on this Leeter Red Dot is so sian. What else to do besides shop, shop, and shop? Hit the road and play Daytona lor!

With vehicles being so urgent to our kiam chye mia, their prevalence in how we talk about life is only to be expected. A lao Singlish word related to them is "gostan". Last time bus conductors would shout this to get a driver to reverse one. "Gostan" is a corruption of "go astern", an instruction used in *sailing*. Dun ask unker how come sailing word can become driving word hor.

Nowsaday, you may still hear driving instructors and co-drivers use "gostan". But you are lagi likely to hear it in contexts of peepur retracting their words or plans reversing course. So, when once our Gahmen got project a population of 6.9 million and then kena widespread kolaveri, it prata-ed and had to gostan on some strategies. "Prata" and "gostan" are same-same but different.

Then we got "langgar", which means collide. You can use this word on vehicles as well as on blur sotongs who on their mobiles all the time and anyhowly jalan. Sibeh kiam pah ler, these kuas! You can scold them until you pumchek – but is no use one. "Pumchek", from the Melayu word "pancit", is another vehicular word, but we got a whole chapter discussing it liao.

From NS, we manly men learn a lot of vehicular terms which we then take back to our civvie lives and infect everybawdy else. For example, peepur dun get into a SUV; they load up macam cargo. They dun alight; they unload or debus, even from a bicycle. By the way, do you know this stupiak Singlish joke about how every Sinkie got two cars? A left ka and a right ka. At their back is the ka chng. Army joke. Funny not funny.

All these terms are kinda commonplace liao. But there is "uplorry", which got start popping out agak-agak in the 2000s nia. "Uplorry", which translates from the Hokkien "ki chia", sounds straightforward lah. But the Hokkien form bo specify what kind of vehicle while our Singlish one does – corrightly. So, in this case, the borrower's word is acherly more zhun than the source wor!

Both "ki chia" and "uplorry" go beyond just getting up a truck. As unker oredi got say so, you dun normally, let alone regularly, uplorry. What you do is load up. You load up a taxi or even a MRT train. You dun uplorry things either, whether they be cargo or your own barang-barang. You cannot uplorry ayams lah, lembus lah, babis lah – but *they* can uplorry one. Their state of being can change.

Blur yet? How we use lorries in Singapore may give a clue to this word's context. Lorries are often used to transport what? Goods, animals, and migrant workers – although can we do something about that last category oredi? Not safe ler! But there is one more use: in a cheena funeral procession, a lorry is oso a hearse with cantik or lawa trimmings. "Uplorry", in this sense, connects with having dieded and then being sent off.

More context: Lao Bengs can tell you how the term oso invokes last time gang fights one. Lorries used to be preferred transport for groups of Ah Bengs to head to secret locations and settle scores with rival gangs. What they then did was hoot one another with parangs, tekkos, and fists like siow lor. To hoot is to beat up. Yes, in Singapore, hooters dun mean same-same as in the US. (In short, dun ask for hooters hor.)

So now loading up onto a lorry should give you a lagi clear idea liao. It does not just describe a tragedy but oso peepur kena seriously or mortally wounded from all the hooting. Because some Ah Bengs got tio until jialat-jialat, they must be carted away in what ang mohs call a dead wagon, a vehicle that collects bodies to bring to the hospital or morgue. "Uplorry" thus got this sense of finality, trauma, and emptiness!

HAMPALANG
UPLORRY
SIOL.

GWEE

The word is both a verb and an adjective. When Ah Kong matied in 2015, he uplorried – or "he uplorry" oso can. You oso dun really need to conjugate the verb form. You can say my pet anjing uplorries, is uplorry-ing, or uplorried, or you can just say "uplorry". You can keep to the same form for both the singular and the plural. Both "My anjing uplorry" and "My two anjings uplorry" oso corright.

It can summore be used to mean how a plan or event habis, causing something to la tee too or some-one to gek sim. So a plan to build a columbarium in a HDB neighbourhood uplorry, and some Sim Lim shop uplorry customers before it ownself uplorry. You can oso use this word on trends whose downturn somehow cannot upturn. So pollution index lah, property prices lah, the ringgit lah, cryptos lah, can uplorry too.

The beauty of "uplorry" is it reminds us of how vehicles are not means to get from Point A to Point B nia. They are so much a part of our sian Sinkie lives that they are oso the transport of *death*. Be it a hearse or an Ah Beng truck, the lorry conjures a cultural image of life's inconsequence. Unker dun see this nuance going away anytime before we can acherly stop using lorries to transport peepur! (Hinting again.)

So let ang mohs have their mythical boat of Charon to ferry matied folks to the other world. We Sinkies got our trusted lorry, and it is lagi powderful because its everyday visibility serves as a reminder of how life can piak just liddat. Life is sibeh fragile one. Some day, each of us will oso be loading up that lorry on our last lawa journey to where we all kena saman for the way we have driven our lives.

~~GROSSERLY~~ GLOSSARY

Hampalang Singlish words and phrases used in this book are listed here. Those with more than one entry mean they are completely different terms with just the same speowling. Words originating in other languages are given Singlish definitions nia.

2359: army book-in time
4D: lottery

A SCREW LOOSE: crazy
ABC: American-born Chinese
ABERDEN: what do you expect
ACHERLY: actually
ACTION: showy

Glossary

AGAK-AGAK: roughly

AGONG: king

AH: and

AH: a filler

AH BENG: uncouth Chinese boy

AH BOI: boy

AH GONG: idiot

AH KONG: grandfather; Lee Kuan Yew

AH LAO: adult; senior

AH LIAN: uncouth Chinese girl

AH LONG: loan shark

AH LOONG: Lee Hsien Loong

AH MA: grandmother

AH PUI: fat person

AH TER AH KOW: Tom, Dick, and Harry

AI SAY: wow

AI ZAI: keep cool

AIYOH: a groan

AIYOYO: a groan

AKSI BORAK: show off

ALAMAK: oh dear

ANG KONG: picture

ANG MOH: white person

ANG MOH PAI: Westernised class

ANGER: angry

ANGKAT BOLA: ingratiate oneself

ANJING: dog
ANNAN: elder brother
ANNEH: elder brother
ANOT: or not
ANYBAWDY: anybody
ANYHOW-ANYHOW: anyhow
ANYHOWLY: anyhow
APA INI: what is this
ARM CHIO: quietly pleased
ATAS: superior; uppity
AUNTIE: middle-aged woman
AUTA: lousy
AYAM: chicken

BABI: pig
BAGUS: good
BAK CHEW: eyes
BALIK: back
BALIK KAMPUNG: go home; get lost
BANANA: Westernised Chinese person
BANGANG: stupid
BARANG-BARANG: belongings
BATU: stone
BEDEK: bluff
BEO: ogle at
BEST: most extreme

Glossary

BESTEST: most excellent

BLUR: clueless; confused

BLUR-BLUR: semi-consciously

BLUR SOTONG: clueless or confused person

BO: without; don't have

BO CHUP: not care

BO LANG: nobody

BO LAT: feeble

BO TAK CHEK: uneducated

BODOH: fool

BODOH PEH KAMBING: fool

BOI: boy

BORN AND BLED: born and bred

BRUDDER: brother

BUAY: cannot; fail to

BUAY SONG: disgruntled

BUAY TAHAN: can no longer tolerate

BUAY ZAI: not in control; wobbly

CABUT: run away

CALEFARE: extra

CAMPUR: mix

CAMPUR-CAMPUR: keep mixing

CAN: capable; good enough; permitted

CAN DUN: can you not

CANNOT MAKE IT: substandard

CANTIK: pretty; lovely

CATCH NO BALL: cannot understand

CCA: Co-Curricular Activities

CEPAT-CEPAT: hurry up

CHAMPION: standout

CHAPALANG: assorted

CHAR BOR: woman

CHEE KO PEK: dirty old man

CHEEM: deep; profound

CHEENA: Chinese

CHEWREN: children

CHIN CHYE: not fussy

CHIO: beautiful

CHIO BU: beautiful woman

CHIONG: charge; get wasted

CHOP-CHOP KALIPOK: hurry up

CHOW KUAN: unscrupulous

CHOW MUGGER: disgustingly diligent student

CHOW MUGGER TOAD: most disgustingly diligent student

CHOW TURTLE: disgusting person

CHUM: miserable

CHUM-CHUM: mix

CHUT: come out

CHUT PATTERN: resort to tricks

CIVVIE: civilian

COCK: nonsense

COCKANATHAN: nonsense; idiot

COKLAT: chocolate

CONFIRM-PLUS-CHOP: guaranteed

CONSPERM: confirm

CORRIGHT: correct

COW-PEH: shout

COW PEH COW BU: shout

COW SENSE: common sense

CPF: Central Provident Fund

CUCUK: taunt

CUM: with

DEBUS: alight

DEEN: didn't

DEY: hey

DI DI: younger brother

DIAM: keep quiet

DIAM-DIAM: quietly

DIEDED: died (past participle)

DOUBLE-CONFIRM: re-confirm

DOWAN: don't want

DRAMA: dramatic

DUH: dull-witted

DUMB-DUMB: stupid

DUN: don't

DUN PLAY-PLAY: don't fool around; don't underestimate
DUNNO: don't know

ECA: Extra-Curricular Activities
EET: it (emphasis)
EEYER: yuck
EH: a filler; hey
EH ZHO NANG: can be humane
ELAK: avoid
ENG: free
ENGLAND: English
ESKEW ME: excuse me
EVERYBAWDY: everybody
EXCUE: excuse
EXERSAI: exercise

FASTERLY: quickly
FAST-FAST: quickly
FEWL: feel
FEWLING: feeling
FILEM: film
FLY KITE: get lost
FRIEND-FRIEND: make friends
FRUS: frustrated
FUNNY NOT FUNNY: joke in poor taste

Glossary

GABRA: panic

GAHMEN: government

GARANG: brave

GASAK: act quickly

GASAK BUTA: make wild guesses

GEDDIT: get it

GEENA: child

GEERO: zero

GEK SIM: heartbroken

GERAM: resentful

GEREK: awesome

GIAN: greedy in little ways

GILA: crazy

GILA MONSTER: crazy person

GOBLOK: stupid

GOLI: marble; game of marbles

GONE CASE: lost cause

GONG: ignorant

GONG-GONG: ignorant

GOONDU: idiot

GOSTAN: reverse

GOTONG ROYONG: communal cooperation

GST: Goods and Services Tax

GUAI-GUAI: obedient

GUNUNG: mountain

HA: for expressing caution

HABIS: finished

HALF PAST SIX: lackadaisical

HAMPALANG: all

HANTU: ghost

HAPPENING: fashionable; vibrant

HAPPY LIKE BIRD: chirpy; contented

HAPPY-HAPPY: happily

HAYWIRE: off course

HDB: Housing and Development Board

HELIUCATED: educated

HELPCHOO: help you

HENG: lucky

HENG AH: thank goodness

HENTAM: whack

HEOW: wild

HIGH-HIGH: very high

HO SAY: good

HO SAY BO: how are you

HOOT: beat up

HOR: for expressing irritation

HOW LIAN: boast

HUAT: gain; prosper

HUM-TUM: whack

HUNGER: hungry

IBU: mother
IPPT: Individual Physical Proficiency Test
IRREGARDLESS: regardless
ISD: Internal Security Department

JAGA: guard
JALAN: walk
JALAN-JALAN: a stroll
JIAK KENTANG: Westernised; Westernised person
JIALAT: terrible
JIALAT-JIALAT: a serious extent

KA: leg
KA CHNG: backside
KACANG: peanut
KACAU: irritate
KAKA: monster
KAKI: buddy
KALIPOK: curry puff
KAPO: grab
KAPO KING: pilferer
KAWAN-KAWAN: friends
KAY: fake
KAY ANG MOH: proudly Westernised person
KAY KIANG: smart-alecky
KAY SIAN: very bored

KAY-KAY: pretend

KENA: get

KENA SAI: get shat on

KENGSTER: skiver

KESIAN: pity

KETUK: knock; cheat

KI CHIA: die

KI SIOW: go crazy

KIAM: stingy

KIAM CHYE MIA: worthless life

KIAM PAH: deserve a beating

KIASU: afraid of losing

KILAT: excellent

KIO: called

KOLAVERI: rage

KONG SIMI: what do you mean

KOON: sleep

KOPE: capture

KOPI: coffee

KOPITIAM: coffeeshop

KOR KOR: elder brother

KOSONG: zero

KOTEK: penis

KOYAK: damaged; inferior

KUA: fool; clown

KUA KUA: a sigh of disappointment

KUAI LAN: rascally
KUAT: strong
KUCING: cat
KUKUJIAO: idiot; rascal
KUM SIA: thank you
KUNJI: penis

LA-DEE-DA: casual; oblivious
LA TEE TOO: perished
LAGI: even more
LAH: for emphasis or enumeration
LANGGAR: collide
LAWA: gorgeous
LAO: old
LAO BENG: uncouth Chinese men
LAO HONG: gone stale
LAO KWEE: embarrassed
LAO SAI: have diarrhoea
LAO YA: lousy
LAST TIME: long ago; at one time
LAWA: gorgeous
LEETER: little
LEETER RED DOT: Singapore
LEH: come on
LEMBU: cattle
LEMBEK: flaccid

LEPAK: chill

LER: do you know

LIAO: already; finished

LIDDAT: like that

LIDDIS: like this

LIM: drink

LIM KOPI: face interrogation

LOAD UP: get on

LOBANG: hole; opportunity

LONG-LONG: very long; long ago

LONGKANG: drain

LOR: for expressing resignition

LOR SOR: longwinded

LOTI: bread

LOUD-LOUD: loudly

LOW CRASS: low class

LUAN: out of control; chaotic

LUGI: lose; lose out

LUMBER: number

MABOK: drunk

MACAM: like

MAGGI MEE: curly hair

MAH: don't you know

MAI HIAM: hold the chilli

MAI HUM: hold the cockles

MAI ZHO KANG: refuse to work

MAI TU LIAO: don't wait any longer

MAKAN: food; eat

MALU: embarrass; embarrassing

MALUATING: embarrassing

MAMA: uncle

MAT: Malay man

MAT SALLEH: Westerner

MATI: die

MATIED: died; dead

MEDISAVE: a medical savings scheme

MEE SIAM MAI HUM: a glaring blunder

MEH: for expressing doubt

MEI MEI: younger sister

MELAYU: Malay

MINISTAR: minister

MISUNNERSTAN: misunderstand

MO TAK TENG: incomparable

MONYET: monkey; troublemaker

MUG: study

MUGGER: diligent student

MUGGER TOAD: disgustingly diligent student

MUM-MUM: food

NANTI: wait

NEH: what about

NEH: never

NEMMIND: never mind

NGEH-NGEH: persistently

NGEOW: fussy

NIA: only

NO BIG NO SMALL: rude; disrespectful

NOBAWDY: nobody

NONID: no need

NOTCHYET: not yet

NOTTI: naughty

NOWSADAY: nowadays

NS: National Service

OBASAN: tackily dressed auntie

OBIANG: out of fashion

OCCIFER: army officer

ON: we have an agreement

ONCE A PONG A TIME: once upon a time

ONZ: we have an agreement

ORANG PUTIH: white person

ORBIGOOD: serves you right

OREDI: already

OSO: also

OT: work overtime

OWNSELF: on one's own; personally

PAISEH: shy; embarassed
PAK TOR: dating
PAKAY: legitimate
PALLY-PALLY: on friendly terms
PANCHAN: pardon; give chance
PANCIT: punctured
PANDAI: clever
PANG KANG: finish work
PAP: People's Action Party
PARANG: machete
PATTERN: tricks
PECAH: break; broken
PECAH LOBANG: wreck a scheme
PEEPUR: people
PIA: rush; work hard
PIAK: slap; break
PIAK-PIAK: have sex
POK KAI: broke
POOT: fart; f**k
POSB: Post Office Savings Bank
POTONG STIM: party-poop
POWDERFUL: powerful
PRATA: flip-flop
PUI-PUI: fat
PUKI: vagina
PUMCHEK: exhausted; deflated

PUNDEK: vagina

RA: adults only
REPORK: report
RILEK: relax
ROJAK: mix
ROTI: bread
RUGI: lose; lose out

SABO: sabotage
SABO KING: nuisance
SAF: Singapore Armed Forces
SAI: shit
SALAH: wrong
SAMAN: summons
SAMA-SAMA: similarly; together
SAME-SAME: alike
SAME-SAME BUT DIFFERENT: superficially alike
SAR KAR: ingratiate oneself
SAYA TAK TAHU: I don't know
SAYANG: love; cherish; empathise with
SCULLY: what if
SEDAP: delicious
SEE NO UP: look down on
SEKALI: what if
SELAMAT PAGI: good morning

SENGET: crooked

SHACK: extremely tired

SHIOK: amazing

SHIOKANATHAN: amazing; sensation

SHOW FACE: dare to be present

SI: die

SI GEENA: brat

SIAL: for expressing incredulity

SIAM: avoid; move aside

SIAN: boring; bored

SIAN: dupe

SIAN: celestial being

SIAN JIT PUAH: very bored

SIAN TOW: braggart

SIANZ: boring; bored

SIBEH: very

SIKIT: a little

SIMI: what

SIMI SAI: whatever matter

SIMI SAI OSO POLITISAI: politicise anything and
    everything

SIMPER: simple

SINKIE: Singaporean

SIO: piping hot

SIOL: for expressing incredulity

SIONG: tough

SIOW: crazy

SIOW TING TONG: crazy person

SOFT-SOFT: softly

SOMEBAWDY: somebody

SONG: amazing

SOTONG: squid; clueless or confused person

SPEOWL: spell

SPEOWLING: spelling

SPEOWLT: spelt

SPIAK: speak

SPIAK: flamboyant

STAND-BY: inspection

STEADY: impressive

STEADY POM PI PI: well done

STEADY POON PEE PEE: well done

STIM: stimulating

STIR: provoke

STUNNED LIKE VEGETABLE: dumbfounded

STUPIAK: stupid

STYLO-MILO: stylish

SUAN: taunt

SUKA: like

SUKA-SUKA: as one pleases

SUMMORE: some more

SUMPAH: swear; promise

SUAY-SUAY: unluckily

SURPLISE: surprise
SUSAH: difficult
SYIOK: amazing
SYOK: amazing

TAK CHEK: study; educated
TAKE COVER: hide
TALK COCK: talk nonsense
TALK COCK SING SONG: talk nonsense
TAO: aloof
TEKKO: pole
TEMBAK: shoot
TERBALIK: the other way round
TERIMA KASIH: thank you
TERRIHORBLE: terribly horrible
TERUK: nasty; tough
TERUK-TERUK: to a nasty extent
TETEK: tits
THAMBI: younger brother
THANI: drink
THIN-THIN: very thin
THNG CHU: go home
THUR: stupid
TIDAK APA: lackadaisical
TIDUR: sleep
TIKAM-TIKAM: pick at random

TIO: get
TIO BO: am I right
TIO CHUAK: shocked
TOK KONG: important
TOLONG: a plea for help
TOMBALIK: the other way round
TOWKAY: business owner
TUA KI: powerful; influential
TUA POW SIAN: braggart
TUAN-TUAN DAN PUAN-PUAN: ladies and gentlemen

UGERLY: ugly
UNKER: middle-aged man
UNLOAD: alight
UNNERSTAN: understand
UNNERSTOODED: understood (past participle)
UPLORRY: die
USE YOUR BRAIN: put in some thought
UTANG: owe

VERY THE: very
VOMIT BLOOD: exasperated

WAH: a cry of wonder
WAH SAY: wow
WAH PIANG EH: for goodness's sake

WAIT: what if

WAKE UP YOUR IDEA: snap out of it

WALAO EH: for goodness's sake

WALLOP: beat up; eat heartily

WAN: want

WAN AN: good night

WAYANG: staged performance

WHACK: beat up; eat heartily

WOR: for expressing surprise

WORLD-CRASS: world-class

YAYA: arrogant; aloof

ZAI: cool

ZEN: stoic

ZHO KANG: work

ZHO SIAN: live without a care

ZHO SIMI: what are you doing

ZHUN: accurate

ABOUT THE AUTHOR CUM ILLUSTRATOR

GWEE LI SUI suka write lah, draw lah, talk cock sing song lah. He got publish many kilat books from poetry books and comic books to critical guides and lite-ra-ry anthologies. You got buy any of those? Bo, corright? That is why he must now oso make Singlish books lor. Other than *Spiaking Singlish*, he got translate world classics into Singlish, such as Antoine de Saint-Exupéry's *The Leeter Tunku*, Beatrix Potter's *The Tale of Peter Labbit*, and the Brudders Grimm's fairy tales. This unker sibeh siow on one!